Forward:

    This book is dedicated to the people in the world who want more and the best out of life. The people who are ready for change. First, I want to start this journey off the right way and can't continue without giving thanks and love to God for my life, the priceless lessons, and unforgiveable strength. The relationship has changed my life from a lost young man to a man with a vision and purpose who's determined to complete my assignment before I leave this earth. Secondly, I want to thank to my wonderful parents (Revie and Herbert) for unconditional love, guidance, and support throughout my life. Your presence in my life means a lot more than I can ever express physically or mentally; however, I'll continue to try and show how much I truly care and love you both. Thirdly, I'm thankful for my younger sister (Hertira) and older brother (Herbert). Both of you truly keep me balance in this thing we call life, and I always listen more than you might think. Finally, I must give a very very big shout out to my queen (Jasmine) and son (Romalis). I never gave this much love away so easily in life. One of the only reason I do it is because you both put me in a real safe sincere place. I remember praying on my knees at the age of 17 years old asking God for a girl who truly loves me and will understand where you're about to take me and in return God gave me a beautiful queen that's loyal to me, sticks with me through my highs and lows, and blessed me with a young king. I'm forever grateful for my life.

Chapter 1 (W.A.R)

First before we get into the necessary steps it takes of becoming a first-time home owner. We must first have the W.A.R mindset. W.A.R. is an abbreviation I created once after looking back on my journey and taking away all the ingredients for my success. You'll first develop the W.A.R mindset and after applying, fully understanding the concept, and achieving your goals. It'll then change to a lifestyle motto to follow on anything you're pursing in your life. I'm pretty sure you're ready to know what the abbreviation stands for and I'm ready to give you the ingredients. The reason I'm excited to let you know is because this W.A.R. mindset is the exact reason I was able to invest in my first real estate property at the age of 20 years old. Wow 20 years old? How did you do that? Where did you start? Did your parents buy it for you? These are the questions I get when I tell people about my story. Well there was no financial handout given from my family, and no one in my network who gave me the needed steps. I was a student throughout the whole public-school system who struggled, and I'm sure this is not your first-time hearing this from someone. I was a young man who constantly doubted myself and didn't have a strong relationship with God. I felt as if I had no light or possibilities within for me. The main reason for me telling you this is to show you that you don't need to be smart, unique, or talented. You want to know the first thing you need? You need to BELIEVE. If you can believe and see it, then you can have it. I'm not telling you something to make you feel good I'm telling you something that I did, and it worked. I will increase and then challenge your belief level before the chapter is over so get ready.

The abbreviation for W.A.R means Willing, Able, and Ready. Let's dive more in depth. First, **you must be willing to do what others won't**. Yes, willing to wake up early in the morning head to the gym for a good workout. Willing to wake up and cook a healthy breakfast rather than going through a fast-food drive thru. Willing to sacrifice 30 minutes out of your day and read a book to strengthen your temporary weakness. Willing to get out of your comfort zone and get uncomfortable with your fears. Remember .. **You can't change what you refuse to confront**. Stop for a moment and think about a few times when you were afraid of doing something. Now I want you to choose one of those times when you had no choice but to get uncomfortable, and after doing so you found out it wasn't bad as you thought. Today, your past uncomfort zone is a comfort zone for you because of your *will* to confront it. What do we most encounter before being willing. Most of the time we suffer from fear of making the first step. Let's attack this thing we call fear and make sure whenever it comes in our life we know exactly the true meaning of it. F.E.A.R means False Evidence Appearing Real. Please understand the true meaning and after be willing to take the first step. When a child learns to walk and falls 50 times, they never think to themselves: "maybe this isn't for me?" It was very uncomfortable for you to walk, however look at you now. For a second, just think about how much you get done in life by just walking. What if you never got uncomfortable with walking as a baby? Can you imagine being an adult crawling around? Wow! I'm sure you get the point by now and I know you have the will power to get the job done.

Secondly, **you must be able to mentally endure temporary failure and pain**. There's one question you should ask yourself before continuing the process. Am I mentally able to endure temporary failure and pain? Yes, you might be physically qualified to do the job, but not mentally able to survive it. It's not always about who can run the fastest but more about who can make it to the end of the race. If you want to have the best positive mindset possible on your journey, quickly change failure and pain to feedback. Why? Because when you think about failure it brings unhappiness and stress. Also, when you think about pain it brings discomfort and suffering. After these two words collaborate we then connect to the wrong emotions which causes our mind to go crazy. Try to replace failure and pain with feedback. Because that's simply what we're getting back after trying to do anything. Getting feedback from an attempt is one of the best things to get back in return. How would you know what you're getting without feedback? The feedback you get back is your score card. If your score is low, then you know there's work to be done. After acknowledging your score card, you should always brainstorm ways to improve your score. Why? Because who wants to keep or even have a low score card in life. YOU ARE IN CONTROL of improving your life in many ways. You must sacrifice some time, find ways to increase your score quickly, and do them. Now that you know to replace failure and pain to feedback. Getting feedback is the best return after making any attempt. Thereafter, examine your score card and make the proper adjustments to improve it.

Thirdly, you must be ready to take the first step. This is the most vital stage of the process because if you don't do this, then everything was pointless and doesn't matter. Ready defines in a suitable state for an activity, action, or situation; fully prepared. Being willing and able should put you in a suitable state for action to take place next. The action is what made Martin Luther King Jr. the most visible spokesperson and leader in the Civil Rights Movement. Dr. King wasn't just talking about issues in the country however more about action. He traveled to the White House to speak with the President of the United States of America about Civil Rights. He also led a non-violent march into Selma, Alabama, for getting equality for colored people. Without action you will have a difficult time accomplishing anything. Having a plan with no action involved is like having a car full of gas in parked and never putting the car in drive. There's a quick story that one of my greatest mentors told me about a little boy named Michael! It was a beautiful day at school and Michael was at recess with a group of other kids. The school bell was about 10 minutes from ringing for reporting back to class. The other kids created a game called "who can jump and make it to the tree?" All the other kids were excited and were lining up for their big jump. The distance between the starting point to the tree was about 4 feet away when the time came to jump, one kid asked Michael where does it he want to jump? Because of the curious look on his face. Michael answered saying" I want to jump pass the water puddle". The water puddle was about 4 feet away from the tree but not for Michael's W.A.R mindset. The other kid told Michael " you can't jump that far that's impossible". Michael answered, " Even if I don't make it pass the water puddle I will pass everybody else who's jumping for the tree". Moral of the story is dream big with the W.A.R. mindset because even if you don't get to make it to your water puddle at least you're ahead of everybody else who's focus on the tree. ARE YOU READY? ARE YOU SURE? OK THEN LET'S GO!!!

This is an exercise that will make your vision more visible to you. I want you to print a picture of your first property and put it here:

Chapter 2: If You Can Rent, Then You Can Own

Why should you become a first-time homeowner? The reason is because if you can rent and pay your landlord, then you can own and pay the mortgage company. Stop and think about it for a second ... What does it take to rent the average apartment? First, you must be able to show proof of income from your job (usually recent paystubs or bank statements). Secondly, you must complete a background check. Thirdly, nowadays you must do a credit check for financial worthiness because who wants to rent to someone who owes everybody. Fourthly, you must be able to provide the required deposit amount. Lastly, you must sign the lease agreement for the terms chosen. Most people go through all these steps and rent forever without owning a square foot of the property. One reason I became a homeowner is because I felt I would be paying too much money to a person that will never give me the deed to the property.

Why pay someone forever and never receive ownership? For example, you have Michael (the renter) who lived at 188 Dolphin State Street for 7 years and still counting. Mr. Thompson (the landlord) leases the property for $1000 per month to Michael. Mr. Thompson purchased the house for $80,000 dollars and pays the bank $700 per month for the mortgage payment. It's common sense to see what Mr. Thompson is doing; however, let me explain he's simply taking the $1,000 dollars from Michael. Thereafter, he pays the $700 dollars to mortgage company and still has a remaining positive cash flow of $300 monthly. This is where it gets tricky and confusing because Michael has been living at 188 Dolphin Street for 7 years. So, the four questions are, how much money has Michael paid Mr. Thompson so far? Michael has paid Mr. Thompson $84,000 dollars. Does Michael get ownership of the property because he paid more than what it's worth? The answer is no, Michael doesn't get ownership he continues to pay $1,000 per month. WOW? Is this legal? Yes, it's legal and called principal pay down which is the system Mr. Thompson is operating under. One way to use principal paydown is when the mortgage borrower (Mr. Thompson) gets a tenant (Michael) to pay the principal and interest of the mortgage. In doing so, the tenant(Michael) is paying down Mr. Thompson debt. Last question when Michael leaves the house and goes buy his home ... Does he get any of the money back out of the total amount paid to Mr. Thompson? No, he doesn't the only thing Michael may get back is his initial deposit. This is the operation happening with many houses, apartments, and condos.

    I'm here to change the theory that renting is the cool thing to do into owning your first home is the smartest thing to do. Becoming a homeowner is a similar process of becoming a tenant however there's a little more vital requirements which we will cover throughout the chapters to come. You deserve to be the owner of your residence when you're putting the hard-earned hours into your business or job. There's many benefits of becoming a homeowner such as power and control, tax benefits, appreciation, and equity. When you become a homeowner you instantly have power and control over your property and can legally do whatever you want to do. If you have family members who are visiting or need a place to live because of temporary circumstances, you have the power and control to make the decision. Usually you must ask or give the landlord/property manager a notice about the upcoming activity. It's a good feeling to be able to be in control of your land and not have to ask permission for doing the right thing.

Another powerful thing you have is power and control over the air rights above your property. What? Yes, you heard right when you become the homeowner not only do you own the land on the ground but also the air rights above it. Meaning, at any given time you can sell the air space above your property. Usually these transactions take place in the downtown area with commercial real estate. Tax breaks are another great benefit you get of becoming a home. If you use your home purely as your personal residence, you cannot deduct the cost of home improvements. These costs are nondeductible personal expenses. However, this doesn't mean that home improvements do not have a tax benefit. This is because the cost of home improvements is added to the tax basis of your home. Your house payment may include several costs of owning a home. The only costs you can deduct are real estate taxes that qualifies as home mortgage interest, and mortgage insurance premiums. How does home ownership affect taxes? It is a form of income that is not taxed. Homeowners may deduct both mortgage interest and property tax payments as well as certain other expenses from their federal income tax. Appreciation is one of the best things about being a homeowner because is it a great way to increase the value of your asset. Overtime the property has a great chance of appreciating especially if the market momentum is increasing because of trending activity. For example, you purchase a property for $80,000 and within the next 5 years the property is worth $100,000. So, based upon this example you would have a guaranteed estimated $20,000 dollar of equity. Also, by 5 years you would've made monthly mortgage payments overtime which makes the amount owed decrease which add more equity into the property. What's Equity? Equity is very important because it's the difference between the current fair market value of the property and the amount the owner still owes on the mortgage. This gives you a lot of leverage because you can now use your first asset to create more assets. You can take out up to 85% of home equity loan or cash out-refinance of the total amount equity. Once you receive the big checks you can now go make home improvements to increase home appreciation, buy a new car, or invest in income producing assets. You now understand why becoming a homeowner is the best and right choice to make as soon as possible in your life.

Calculate how much rent you've paid so far:

<u>Step 1:</u> Rent Amount $ (Per Month) X 12 Months (Yearly Amount) = Total of Yearly Rent Amount

Example: $1,000 × 12 = $12,000

<u>Step 2:</u> Total of Yearly Rent Amount X How Many Years You've Been Renting = Total Amount of Money You've Paid So Far

Example: $12,000 x 10 = $120,000

1. How much money did you pay so far?

_____

2.) How much are you willing to pay to rent until you become a first-time homeowner?

_____

Chapter 3: Your First Enrollment

When beginning your journey of becoming a first-time homeowner you want to first enroll into the first-time homeowner's course. Why first? Because you will learn and understand so much about the process which will put you way ahead of the game, making the process go smoother. Mostly every city offers the course that you can complete and receive a certificate afterwards. You want to browse the internet for " first time homebuyer's course ". One great thing about taking the class is that you'll receive a certificate to give to first time homebuyers assistance programs. These programs have requirements like any other intuition, and one of them is a certificate honoring the completion of hours. If you're interested in financing a property with 2 - 4 units then you'll also have to complete a landlord course. This landlord course will have you ready for any tenant, provide financial management, and guidance on legal actions for eviction. Why take these courses? Because like I mentioned at the beginning of the chapter this will give you needed education and put you ahead of the game. Fortunately, the universe was working in my favor and the timing was just right because the courses were available for me to attend. I enrolled in my courses while in the middle of my financing because I had a good credit score and the eligible income however the only thing I didn't have was the needed certificate for getting a soft second loan. That's exactly why it's important to get this step completed as soon as possible to prevent the same mistake I made.

Soft second loans is one-way state governments can increase home ownership. This is a second mortgage with an interest rate often below the market rate. Soft mortgages solve two of the biggest obstacles first time homebuyers face: making the down payment and paying the closing costs. I received $20,000 dollars for my soft second mortgage, and I never had to make a payment on it, if I follow the rules and regulations. Every program has different guidelines; for example, a few of the most important rules to follow was that I couldn't sell the property in the first 5 years and must remain at my primary residence within those same years. The timing is perfect for writing this book because I just finished my audit with my soft second mortgage and was required to show the last month electrical bill and current homeowners and flood insurance with my name and the property address on it. When I received the letter, it came with a 5-business day letter request for all the documents and if not received, then the loan will not be forgiven. When the loan is not forgiven then you now create debt with monthly payments until the full balance is paid. Obeying by the rules are vital for remaining successful with your first-time property. You shouldn't just want to have an accomplishment of getting the property, but mainly keeping it.

Once you enrolled into the courses within your state you will be given a date when class will begin. You will love the environment so much because it's going to be filled with like-minded individuals who want the same exact thing you want. WHAT'S THAT? TO BE A FIRST TIME HOMEBUYER. It's a good thing because you and other classmates will have similar traits such as willing, able, and ready for the journey. Don't be shy or hesitant to communicate with others there because it a good time to leverage the network you're in. For example, I met a gentleman there who surprisingly was my supervisor's son at my past job as a plumber. He was in the phase of now having a real estate agent look for his property. At the time, I already had a good agent looking for a property on my behalf; however, if I didn't have one then this would've been a great resource moving forward for me to use that referral for success. Sometimes you will have special guest speakers attending class such as real estate agents and homeowner's insurance agents. This is the perfect time to take as many notes as possible, ask questions, and get their business cards for a great resource in the future. Afterwards, you can ask additional questions if everything doesn't get answered and it's better anyway because it's a one on one conservation now. It's common to leave away from the courses with the certificate, at least one new friend, and a real estate agent which is three great things to move to the next step with. I believe in you, so get up, get out and accomplish this goal as soon as possible.

Where's the nearest first-time homeowner's course held?

_____

When's the next available course?

_____

What's mainly 3 things you learned from your course?

___

How many new friends did you make?

___

How was your experience?

___

Chapter 4: Getting Pre-Qualify

This is the beginning of your journey of becoming a first-time homeowner and the first step you must take. This is a very simple step for anybody to do because it doesn't take much to get pre-qualified in your local area. Nowadays with technology you don't have to even leave your residence to get pre-qualified because of certain websites that allow you to get instant results on your application submitted. However, I would recommend you go into your local bank or mortgage company and get a pre-qualification. Think of this, as if you're going to the doctor before school to get a physical check up to make sure everything is fine. After the check-up the doctor will give you a review and let you know your current situation.

When walking into the building, you want to ask for the loan officer or mortgage broker and they will kindly assist and give you a financial checkup. Loan Officers also referred to as "Mortgage Loan Originators", are people who work for banks and other financial institutions with the main objective to recommend individual and business loan applications for approval. Loan officers specialize in commercial, consumer and mortgage loans. Mortgage brokers acts as an intermediary who brokers mortgage loans on behalf of individuals or businesses. Traditionally, banks and other lending institutions have sold their own products. As markets for mortgages have become more competitive; however, the role of the mortgage broker has become more popular. When going into a traditional bank such as Chase, Capital One, or Regions you will ask and deal directly with a loan officer. Unlike loan officers, mortgage brokers don't work for banks. They operate independently and must be licensed. They charge a fee for their service, which is paid at the closing table. The fee is a small percentage of the loan amount, generally between 1% and 2%. When finally getting to the process of doing your application they'll be four vital things the loan officer or mortgage broker will gather. Your income, assets, employment documentation, and a credit report for assessing the borrower's ability to secure financing.

This checklist is a sample of the required documents and things needed to complete a pre-approval application:

*Most recent paychecks stubs 30 days (most recent and consecutive) *Weekly = 4 pay stubs *Bi weekly = 2 pay stubs *Semi monthly = 2 pay stubs *Monthly = 1 pay stub

*Proof of Child Support (12-month transaction history)

*SSI Award Letter (if applicable)

*Retirement Award Letter or check stub (if applicable)

*W-2 for the 2015-2016

*If you had more than one job for tax years 2015-2016 please provide me: * Name of job *Positions held *Contact number *Start and ending dates

*2 months most recent bank statements for all accounts - (all page)

*Copy of driver's license or state ID

Once you have submitted your checklist items please allow 24 - 48 business hours for the reviewing process; thereafter, they will either give you an approval estimated of what you pre-qualify for or give you a consultation at no cost on the proper steps you need to take for getting financing. Did you know your credit score could impact your ability to qualify for financing? And with the recent credit restrictions, it's more difficult to qualify for financing with a score below 620. The lower your credit score is, then the higher your interest rate will be because you're considered a risky borrower. When entering a loan, you want to have the lowest interest rate as possible, and one way to get it is boosting your credit score much as possible before getting pre-qualified. If your credit score is the major reasoning for not getting qualified, then I would highly recommend hiring a trustworthy credit repair company. Also, did you know your current debt to income ratio can prevent financing? Why is debt to income ratio important? Evidence from studies of mortgage loans suggest that borrowers with a higher debt-to-income ratio are more likely to run into trouble making monthly payments. A debt-to-income ratio (DTI) is one-way lenders (including mortgage lenders) measure an individual's ability to manage monthly payment and repay debts. The 43 percent debt-to-income ratio is important because, in most cases, that is the highest ratio a borrower can have and still get a qualified mortgage however a good debt to income ratio is 36% below. How do I calculate my debt to income ratio? To determine your DTI ratio, simply take your total monthly debt figure and divide it by your income. For example, if your monthly debt costs $2,000 per month and your monthly gross income equals $6,000, your DTI is 33%

Chapter 5: Self Evaluation

After getting pre-qualified you will have tangible proof of your current financial possibilities with the lending intuition. Everyone will have a different situation because of the C.I.A formula (credit, income, and assets). Each of those three things are reviewed by the banks which will determine your pre-qualification amount. It's common sometimes to get pre-qualified, afterwards with a good loan officer explaining to you exactly what is needed next. I want you to gather as much information to gain clarity, make sure everything is covered on your side and simply the best question you can ask is" What steps do I take from here to become a first-time homeowner?" This question will open the floor for the expert to provide their expertise while making the road ahead much clear for you to see the finish line. There can be many outcomes after the pre-qualifying stage; however, everybody should have a plan of action moving forward to become a homeowner. Don't compare your situation to anybody else because if everybody has the same story then life will be boring. You must embrace your temporary feedback and do the required steps to get things done.

If you don't get approved because of you credit score, then ... Guess what? Find a credit repair company, a credit specialist, or do it yourself. Next, if you don't get approved for a desirable amount because of your income then ... Guess what? It's time to become frugal with your first home or get a job that pays more money. The dream property you want market value might be $170,000; however, you only got approved for $125,000. What's the next move with a lower pre-qualified amount? Find a good property within the price range. Still move forward and don't let that stop your journey because there is a property out there with your name on it. Only thing you must do is find it throughout the inventory of properties your real estate agent sends to your email. Lastly, what if you don't get approved because of your debit to income ratio then ... Guess what? You might need to pay the balance down on your credit cards or create another financial plan to decrease your current debt.

Thank God my loan officer gave me the few steps I needed to take for moving forward within my self-evaluation phase. One of the steps I had to take was pay off my jewelry credit card that was maxed out, which increased my credit utilization percentage and debit to income ratio. Fortunately, I was a little financially stable when I went through this process. I lived at home with my mom, so I didn't have a lot expenses after helping around the house. It made things a lot easier too because just think about going through this process yourself while living on your own with all the bills in your name and being told out of nowhere to pay one of your credit cards off for a balance of $300-400 dollars. It will create a financial setback and put things out of place especially if you don't have a sufficient amount in your savings account.

Finally, the last step I personally had to take was raise my middle credit score by a few points due to requirements of soft second mortgage and better interest rates for the FHA loan. Let's slow down and gain clarity on your middle score and FHA Loan. What's my middle score? Mortgage lenders pull credit reports from all three bureaus, Equifax, Experian and TransUnion. Then they compare the 3 credit scores. For instance, if you were buying your first property and you had a 618 with TransUnion, a 585 with Equifax and a 649 with Experian, thus the score in the middle is 618 with TransUnion. What's an FHA loan? An FHA loan is a mortgage insured by the Federal Housing Administration. Borrowers with FHA loans pay for mortgage insurance, which protects the lender from a loss if the borrower defaults on the loan. Typically, most of first time homebuyers use an FHA loan for financing. Here's some benefits for getting an FHA loan:

·Credit qualifying criteria not as strict; Credit scores as low as 580 now qualify for an FHA loan

·Low down payment required; FHA loans generally require as little as 3.5% down on the purchase of a home

·Easy Refinancing – Refinance up to 97.75% of your home's value.

"Self-Evaluation is looking at your progress, development and learning to determine what has improved and what areas still need improvement"

Chapter 6: Finding Your Property

This is one of the most exciting times of your journey when finding your first property. It's a journey because you never know how many properties you'll walk in and out of until you find the right one. There's many ways you can begin your journey for finding your property such as hiring a personal Realtor, negotiating the deal yourself, or through the seller's realtor. It's important to understand the steps to take with each route. Which one is the best for starters? Hiring a personal realtor is my suggestion. Why? Because they're out to sincerely meet your expectations for your property with all good intentions. Also, you don't have to pay them upfront, they will get paid at least 3% commission of the purchase price at the closing table.

Another great part about this stage is you get to interview Realtors and choose the one who will help you the best. Interviewing can seem weird at first if you're not use to it; however, it will save you time with going through multiple realtors who can't successfully find, negotiate, and close the deal. You must pre-qualify and evaluate your realtor before taking any more steps forward. Now, if you wanted to be the first-time homeowner who goes out independently to browse the internet and local area to find your property, then do it. However, you will find some adversity because you're not the expert and expertise will be needed when it comes to being in sync during every phase of closing the deal. It's best to find your realtor before speaking to the seller or their agent. Why? Because their agent works for them and not you, so the agent's best intentions and interest is not in your favor. Not to say that they're going to do something illegal or harm you .. It's just business.

The goal in most cases is to get the most profit as possible with the right plan of action. The seller wants to sell their property for much as the COMPS are in the neighborhood. C.O.M.P.S means a real estate appraisal term referring to properties with characteristics that are like a subject property whose value is being sought. However, your realtor wants to negotiate a low purchase price as possible, get the seller to pay for closing cost, and have equity available after the closing cost. Why would they do all this for you? Because you hired them, and they work for YOU! So again, no matter how nice the property looks to you. Simply write the address down and find a realtor to start the process for you. Once you complete your first-time homeowner's course you'll gain great tips and suggestions to take while going through this process.

There's a couple of things you should know and be ready to explain to your realtor when beginning to find your property. First thing you should know is what location do you plan on buying your first property in. This will be based upon your current or future circumstances such as: are you single, engaged, or married with children. Each of the circumstances come with a different plan of action, and that's why it's important to sacrifice 30 minutes prioritizing your prioritizes. After doing that step, you must find the best location for you or your family. If you have children, then it's important to find great school within your district. A low crime area is important whether it's just you, your spouse, or children there as well. Nobody should feel unsafe and scared in their own neighborhood. While finding the right location be sure to find recommended stores, restaurants, and entertainment activities. Everybody has their own way of doing things and it's important to have certain things such as Wal- Mart nearby and not a small neighborhood store with limited products available. Don't rush to find the location just simply do your due diligence, and it will come to you throughout the journey.   Ok, so now you want to figure out how many bedrooms you need. What backyard size is perfect? Will you need office space? Or always wanted a lounge room for yourself or when family and friends come over? These are the questions you need to ask and answer. They truly get you prepared and organized when finally speaking to your realtor. The two last things you really need to know is what's your budget? What's a reasonable mortgage payment for you? This is the time to really look at your current financial situation and choose a reasonable budget and monthly payment you can handle.

These are some questions you need to answer before talking to your realtor for better assistance:

1.) What's important to you at this point of your life?

_____

_____

2.) What's the best location for my current circumstances? And why?

_____

_____

_____

3.) What do you recommend being near your home?

_____

_____

4.) How many bedrooms do you want?

_____

5.) What is your budget for purchasing the property?

_____

6.) What's a reasonable mortgage payment for you?

Chapter 7: What's Next: After I Find My Property?

In most cases, you will be very excited about finding your property and ready to get the keys in your hand the next day. However, there's two important keys for success you must have to become a first-time homeowner. What's the keys? The keys are patience and belief. If you don't have these two keys, then you most likely won't enjoy your journey. Yes, this is the truth because when buying your first home or any property in general, you must evaluate the deal. In order to evaluate the deal, you must do your due diligence. At this point, you won't be doing any of the due diligence personally however you'll be a part of every step and know the status of any pending dilemmas. This is the time when your team gets in position and use their expertise to get you to the closing table as soon as possible. The realtor you hired will do their due diligence and take care of everything dealing with the property such as putting the house under contract, negotiating the deal, and assist with getting the property home inspections completed. The mortgage banker/ broker you hired will do their due diligence and handle everything on the financing side such as keeping you in sync with the status, asking you for additional needed documents, and getting the deal financed quickly. After finding your property, your realtor will have to put a contract on the property to begin the process. This contract is called " A purchase and sale agreement. A Purchase and Sale (P&S) agreement is a legal document that has been prepared and agreed to by attorneys representing the buyers and sellers in a real estate transaction. Both must agree on certain terms... For example, the seller must not take any other offers from buyers and the buyer must give a deposit to take the property off the market temporary while doing everything possible to apply for a loan within a certain period after the contract is signed. The deposit amount is determined by the seller, I remember paying $100 for my deposit. Which is why I'm recommending you to start putting money into your savings account every week or bi weekly. The reason why is because you will have expenses to pay throughout the deal and need reserves. Reserves are basically money reserved in your bank account to cover the potential mortgage payments for 3 - 6 months. This shows the bank that you are prepare for possible financial hardship and have guaranteed payments beginning your loan term. These are some of other things you will have to pay for depending on your circumstances:

*Pest inspectors: Also called a termite inspection, this visual inspection is conducted by a state licensed professional hired to look for signs of infestation or damage to a structure by wood-destroying pests. Pest inspectors look for:

* Wood-destroying pests, such as termites, carpenter ants, rot fungus and wood-infesting beetles. Typical costs: When part of real estate closing costs, termite inspections run $65-$100 and include a Wood Destroying Insect Report which contains two parts.

*Home inspectors: Home inspections are usually conducted by a home inspector who has the training and certifications to perform such inspections. The average home inspection costs around $315, with condos and small homes under 1,000 sq. ft. costing as little as $200. Larger homes over 2,000 sq ft. will run $400 or more

*Licensed contractors (IF NEEDED): Contractors are hired to make sure your project up to city codes and necessitating repairs or removals if your home is inspected or before the property is sold. In most cases, the inspection is free, and they will provide a list of repairs if needed. I would only hire a contractor after getting the ok from the home inspector. The home inspector will cover a lot of the house and if it's something they can't handle then it's time to get the contractor involve.

*Roofers (IF NEEDED): Roofers are people who has a specialize skill with constructing and repairing roofs. I would recommend you get roofers involve when your contractor can't handle the task.

*Appraiser: An appraiser is one who develops and sets a value upon a specific type of property. On average, the cost of a home appraisal on a single-family home ranges between $300 and $400. The price for an appraisal on a multi-family building starts around $600 but can increase depending on the size of the property.

After your due diligence is completed on your property and everything looks great. The last step to take is getting an appraisal on your property and verified document given to the bank to show proof. You might be thinking how long does it take to close on your house after the appraisal? If the loan officer (LO) have all the documentation need it, the appraisal will be sent to the lender's underwriter and it may take 48 hours (depending on how busy they are), after that it will be sent to the closing department and that may take another 48 hours. In short it may take 3 to 5 days to be ready to close. In the mortgage underwriting process, an underwriter will make sure your financial profile matches your lender's guidelines and loan criteria. Then, your underwriter will make the final decision — to approve or deny your loan request. It took me about 4-5 months to get to the closing table. At times, things felt very shaking and discouraging because it seems as if I wasn't going to close on my property, however what I didn't realize was that this was a big investment and it takes time to get everything checked and finalized. So, don't ever take it personally, it's just the process of underwriting.

<u>Chapter 8: The Closing Table</u>

This is one of the most priceless moments of your journey when finally making it to the closing table. I remember the night before my closing day, I felt like a kid all on Christmas Eve all over again. It was hard sleeping through the night knowing that I will get the keys tomorrow and BE A HOMEOWNER at the age of 20 years old. The feeling is impeccable;

however, you will feel it when your time comes. When will you know your closing day? Your mortgage banker/broker will give you a call. I would highly recommend scheduling the closing date around the 20th or 25th of the month versus the last day of the month, to allow time to address any last-minute problems. Why avoid the last day of the month? If a closing scheduled on the last day of the month is not completed that day, you will have increased closing costs, beginning at the start of the next month. That's because prepaid interest due at closing accumulates throughout the month, but it can be avoided or reduced if the closing is near the end of the month. Typically, the closing will be held at your local title company.

Fortunately, they won't have a lot of people in the room. The only people who will be in the room is the title agent, you and your realtor, the seller and their agent. That's the only people needed to get the job done. The only thing they will be a lot of is paperwork for you to sign. The timing on the paperwork is sure to make your hand fall asleep; it just feels like you're signing your life away. I promise this will be the most paperwork you'll ever sign in your life. This signing will be for a great cause because it's a true testimony of when you go to W.A.R for something you want it's highly probable that it will come to reality. After signing all the paperwork, you will be congratulated with lots of smile in the room and your keys to your new home. Everything will feel surreal. I want to congratulate you now because you are a first-time homebuyer in the making. There's no excuses from this point because you have all the information needed. The only thing you must do from this point is go to W.A.R.

I BELIEVE IN YOU!

www.ingramcontent.com/pod-product-compliance
Lightning Source LLC
Chambersburg PA
CBHW071202240526
45470CB00017B/1239